Icaru

MOLLY DONACHIE

*To Margaret, a poetry-friend
with love
from molly.

May '19*

SPM Publications

London

SPM Publications
Unit 136, 113-115 George Lane, South Woodford,
London E18 1AB, United Kingdom
www.spmpublications.com

First published in Great Britain by SPM Publications – an imprint of
Sentinel Writing & Publishing Company in February 2019.

ISBN 978-0-9935035-7-3

Sentinel Writing & Publishing Company is a style of SPM Publications Ltd.

Set in Garamond 9 – 16 points

This book is dedicated to the memory of my parents, Andrew Gibson and Josephine Brogan, and my brothers Andy and Robert.

Acknowledgements

Grateful thanks to the poetry group at Old Blair and to Moniack Mhor Writing School, and to all who provided encouragement, especially Paula Jennings, Gail Wylie, Joyce Caplan, John Glenday and Jen Hadfield.

Special thanks also to Patrick Poon and Bob Syratt for invaluable computer assistance.

Contents

ICARUS

Sisters under the Skin

The women slouch.
Loops of smoke are hitched at their lips.
They're watching and smiling.

Then one after another
unlatching their arms, swinging their hips,
they're jumping rope with us

in the open street. Are filling their lungs
and the narrow air with whoops and chants
fetched up from before.

Floppy-slippered, clutching their skirts
thigh-high, are grinning
in the watery sunlight.

Re-hab

The dower-house is now the admin. block,
much of it predictably still the same – Georgian windows,
chipped stairs.
The real hospital is at the back, with table-tennis
and the local papers.

The yard fills up from time to time –
the men walking as old men walk, no quarter
given. Fumbling for a smoke
after group therapy or computer training.

Some, you notice, count off the rounds
like travelling salesmen. And some in passing
absent-mindedly pat
the stone horse-artilleryman.

You're as close as it gets, but it's not any good,
they're hard to make out:
shapeless lumps, each stubbier, baggier
than his neighbour.

Don't pause to wonder whether wit of man
has lost its reach,
whether more can be done.
Time is slipping, mountains are crumbling

and somewhere else,
under strengthened glass,
Giacometti's silent skeleton men go on,
endlessly striding. Full of purpose.

Chameleon

He's invisible because he avoids your gaze.
              He's unaccountable, will change his story.

He'll trash the pathways
to his central core, pour out his inventory

of sorrows. But remember yours is the final word
     – amen to clean-edged and courteous –

your task to recognise the sword
that flashed in the sun, then cut him down to this.

The Remains

After all, a small room,
with its finger on its cracked lips:
a chair, well-couched, an ashtray of ash,
photographs on an upper shelf -
this inventory
not what you'd expect.

A wreck yes, a mynah bird squawking
perhaps,
the debris from his heart attacks.
Even, sometimes the case, a drawer brimful
of loose change.

Not this
neat life - folded sheets, a few
bottles of beer, St. Theresa of Carmel hung over
the kitchen bin.
Not the picture that would spring immediately to mind,
if you knew him.

And When It's Finished

And when it's finished, I rise early,
take the dog.
By the old steps, by the small wood
lanced with the light,
reach the top vantage point;

look out as the river sticks to its work,
doubling back to catch the moon
and listen to the city,
its past past saving, yet transcendent;

grieve for it, though I can't in the end
remember it all, the old topography –
the shelters and huts,
the tunnel that lies buried under the hill.

We'd had to try.
The sun rising above the opposite shore
is a pale yellow fist, unique,
secretive.

Scan

The eye crass cool
loitering

and this thing billowy,
tied like a fish.

Think space capsule
turbulence ocean.

Eve's pomegranate
round as a coble.

Think drum tense
tight as an egg.

Think web coalescing
sheer dipping.

Wings spread.

And the pucker of cloth
catching him.

The Human Fraction

His back turned to his watching mother,
the teen-age boy is sculling upriver.

The sun fondles jewelled skin
and the wrist-band, stark against the sun-tan.

The skiff draws level. She lifts her arm
in desperate greeting – his gaze holds firm,

fixed on his course. Then he is past her, powering
round the curve of the river. And glittering

like silver, sinuous as the thumb-mark
on his heel, in one whole rush the waves wash back, back.

Icarus

How many times have I reached through my dreams
to get close to the boy
to touch his strength, will-power, energy?

No more than a boy in a half-glimpsed
half-world,
a place of silence, of slippage and purchase,

of whiteness – the white wings steady,
lifting through space, adamant as an arrow,

their only heed the winds' ghosts that are luring him
upwards.

To escape the cage!
To reap the joy of ice-cold air! It's true. I'll face it

like he did, when he weighed his life
against an ostrich feather

and dared to show how a chance is taken,
how a miracle is fashioned – a leap,

straight out. Not difficult at all.
Not a glance, even.

Man, c. 1492

He stands four-square - bold, clear, no sfumato,
entirely within,
sequestered and finite on a sheet of paper.

But he's pushing himself upward out of
the groundwork,
shaking his lustrous thick blond hair
and testing his limbs,

readying himself before our eyes
to step beyond the Realms of gravity
and dare the serene;
till, hard astern, the Darien peaks,

flattened by distance, will start to fall away –
resumed, re-slotted
into massing fault-lines.

The Ladder

The latitudes were easy. You lugged out
your ladder and counted the sky.

But a ladder will soar if you let it,
won't care where you are.

You can stand at the top and crow
or stand at the bottom and sigh.

But some took their time and fenced in
forever, stopped it galloping away

so hands on the rails and boots
on the rungs could corner

the oceans. They gave you the key.

Solidarity

Do you remember
the shipyards at Gdansk

and Lech Walensa leaning out
to give the crowds his voice?

Do you remember
John McLean
and Bob Crow
and the long march on London Snaketown?
Not little men with puffing pipes.
Giants.

Auntie Feenie's Troy

It's a sorry sight:
the bed skewed, and kilts, belts, trailing dresses
heaped about like piles of junk.

She'll never give up is what it's saying.
Back o the bolster,
back like a whale's,
Feenie's making a stand.

The whole street's watching – social worker,
woman downstairs, man from the paper.
Achilles, mad, clenches his fists,
swears under his breath,

and her so little, so brave, so quivering
with passion,
up for the fight,
her grim grimy milk bottles
shoulder to shoulder on the scuffed linoleum.

Then they're rubbing her knuckles
to soothe her down
and you think about things as they take her away
to the assessment centre –
siege fatigue, the epic battles.

And after a while you think again:
sly eye,
craggy gums,
the wily blue transparent grin.

The size of her!

A Sufficiency

See night nudge sun
to get to its rest –
stream run to its river.

See birds in platoons convene
for the signal.
Each does what it must.

As do fox, mole, the cubs
of the she-bear
after the weaning.

So build a hearth, cap the house
with a stout roof-ridge,
and set a gargoyle to ward off winter.

That's more than enough.

Moon Halo

Dominating the dank, sunk garden and the narrow
path to the kitchen door, the halo-ed moon put
all our peevish thoughts to flight. We stopped, in awe
at such a vision. Happens sometimes, the moon's light

refracting as it travels through high wisps of cloud - cirrus
spread in a puff-ball skirt, a colossal shawl, a cuirass
made from crystalled ice. This circle of unearthly
grandeur hung huge over the town and I thought of lowly

shepherds, biblical kings. Of a halo-ed babe and his
innocent mother. Of all the mothers rising from
a fraught bed to tiptoe in, who'd see it and pause
in wonder. Then turn to check, tuck in an arm

or leg - each child his own, halooing off the steep
cliffs, lording it in the avenues of sleep.

Callum Innes

A judicious line, the colour of corn,
drawn with freedom.

Small honeycombs of black within the stalk –
bees' work long in the making.

The line extends, ushers the eye to the edge
of perception,
leaves it there on the rim of the canvas:

a road to be travelled.

Cezanne at the Courtauld, 2001

Live by the rules, play the cards, you win the game
No tricks like that was what he was thinking.
Though his shoulders must have ached, painting
this footpath by the wooded pond at Osny
when he visited Pissarro.
Yet kept to his task, tracking every twist
and turn till the truth was shining out at him –
the flicker of those tree-trunks like chameleons and those
biscuit-coloured ones slender in the distance
lifting up their green tops to inhale his air.
And later at home quietly in Aix, no more interrogation.
Standing back and squinting.
Setting this flowering plant obliquely on a table
which he'd used before. Next three pears by a windowsill.
Here, deep in the shift and tangle of our life –
these little lives we cleave to.

Houses at Auvers, 1890
(Boston Museum of Fine Arts)

Allow me to enter. Permit me to encounter. Permit me to be terrified.
                    (Paul Klee, diary entry of 1908 for van Gogh)

The little houses crouch on the ridge in a ragged
line. Lie close as turf,
yet each roof counts, oblong against oblong.

Low houses, humble sky - I hang back, ambushed
by a glance of sun.
And my schedule falters.

How could we take on a world gripped, convulsed
by some force in him,
the whipped trees, the violent moons -
a life at stake in every stroke, every stalk of wheat?

But here, the houses have gathered gently
and, glimmering around them
farther and farther, all the fields he loved,
his flights of birds.

My heart shifts.
Permit me to enter.
Here. Without fear. I'll find you.

(Paul Klee, diary entry:
Vincent - a Auvers-sur-Oise decede, a l'age de 37 ans.)

The Country Bus

The house, worse luck,
is surrounded by trees, so the hill-foot's obscured
and you go by the clock.

No, it won't be put off, it looms like thunder,
is ripe with disaster – time's, as always, dangerously
tight (the road-end 300

seconds from here). Vital your nerve doesn't
wilt at the point. The cat won't expire,
the hens won't

suffer. Your conscience can glare or
wag all it wants – one measly turn, one heinous drop
of the hair-trigger

wheel and the arrow will fly, will deny
you the chance to be adequate, real,
properly

glittering. So zip on the rain-hood –
the path round the pond is the back of your hand.
Gravel. Earth. Earth. Grass. Shade –

into the shine of the sun. Run, lass, run.
Cursing your skirt, scurrying like an ant, yelling
like billy-o to flag it down.

The Rivals   After Catullus (Poems 50 and 85)

There was the day
we two spent at a loose end limbering up
on our poetics.

Inveterate scribblers: tweaking verses, flexing form,
testing for pace and pitch
and cadence.

Feverishly I drank your wine,
came home, obsessing still at your happy leaps,
your brilliance.

I could not eat or settle. Conjured your wit,
your riot, your ardent talk.
I baulked; the eastward stars eastward

declined; and these lines at last
I mistily assembled.
If you ask me how - awake,

asleep - I do not know,
am almost indifferent,
almost scorn them.

For they bowed with a tiny particular
cough, like the creak of a door -
and stiff, not brave in the least.

So brittle, my dear,
I couldn't but give up on them.
But they came like love, benevolent.

And I'm torn in two.

My Sonnet

meditates, barely there
at the corner of the screen,
the cat at
the leap on to
a lap,
the dog at the slip.

****

A spitter of rain.
The words are hovering, waiting to fly.
They steal my days,
commandeer my winter nights –
cast-offs
on a tattered page,
marginalia.

In Defence of the Language
(after Yevtushenko, "The Heirs of Stalin")

So, where there's a clear and present danger,
   we ask them

      To double
          To treble
            To quadruple
                 the guard.

Camouflage

A hazy moon, and faces stippled –
since ancient times, we know for a fact, makers of war
have practised deception.

When able to fight, seeming unable –
out gathering the horses, seeming at play.
Gulling, hoaxing a whole city like Troy.

Contraptions in hollows, tarpaulin shrouds
at night, on runways,
pulleys, trip-wires, all the devices all set
for subtraction.

Be deeper. Quicker. Neither
here nor there: think army skulking in Birnam wood,
more flicker than substance.

The watchword: sly. Lie low as a mudworm.
Works like a dream –
consider the hare, ptarmigan, willow-grouse

reclaiming the fields
in the swelling air, their winter's dress reverting
to rich,

their silvery muscles puffed out, potential.
Tricked out
for a new season.

Siamese Girl

To raid her heart as if it were mine.
To flood with her blood.
To lie at her hip, a piece of the Continent,
a part of the main –
that is my lot, my portion.

Lips, saliva, budded tongue die in the wound.
The wound closes over
and with each punctured bone, each boundary
sealed even,
one Island is the closer-woven, another riven.

Yet, who's to say some core, some narrow
anamorphic self
won't slip into a distant half-grown universe,
where death and the obverse of it
may come to certainty - or not,

that Solomon may not be there.
Divided king.
Still weeping on his lonely throne.
Still beating his head, beating the flames back,
holding the rope of the silent bell
                        in his gnarled hand?

Day Waits, Hill-road Lost

Day waits,
  hill-road lost in slipping snow.

Moon hangs on veiled rim.

Loch, weed-trails falling lank, weightless,
  stills.

Still Weather, December 30th

Pale pinks and greys, with muscular blue –
a property of the light.
It's four below, we're heading north,
and suddenly it's another country.

 A wide perspective; a rearing landscape
of bare brown clarity, like Breughel's
winter's day.
Though here, not so busy –

a few farm dogs; and birds, shabby,
dishevelled in the cold;
a hare careering upright, insanely,
along a lowish parapet of hillside.

We stare out from the car: at yews got fat
with numberless summers;
at clumps of oak;
at head-stones meandering ahent a kirk
(the souls called forth generations ago).

 And now, the sky – divisions of silver
and amber and black as black
as Corsican plums,
the light striking through,

stalling the neon of the roadside bar
and making it quiver. We know, for sure,
it's change coming.
You turn over your palm. I smile back –

oh, yes. We owe this day: the landfalls
of light,
this windfall.

Thread

A thread trailing from a jacket hem.
I saw it as he turned to leave.
Un-balanced me.

Then his stance shifted.
Or the light rendered the thread unsee-able.
If I'd said, would he have pondered,

given it a second thought.
The link. The slender cotton swinging
like a spider's work —

that small unravelling.

Four-letter Word

Only a word.
Only a scratching on a folded page.
Will it lie bloodless amongst the others?
Or blaze.

I shrink from it: something deep in me
retreats, misgiving.
And so, glib, at a nib's stroke,
"As ever" on the penultimate line

lays the weighty ghost of "Love".

In the Water with Marilyn Monroe

In a hotel pool in suburban L.A.
(escaping from the killing heat), I sculled about,
nursing my bruises,

was contemplating the lane they keep
for budding nymphs and little babies,
when whoosh!

she leapt up, laughing with delight,
blonde hair flattened,
those eyelashes, those lips

of pure carmine
glistening from the water,
and as she caught her breath and gasped,

her small hands cupped about her face,
that wondrous smile,
half-child, half-siren,

eclipsed everything;

and with a turn of slender shoulder,
a little wiggle of the tail,
she was the mermaid in the beaded dress

who breathed the birthday song to Mr. President
and a dazzled world.

I Can Hardly Believe

I can hardly believe they're shining
so brightly outside my window
as the radio plays.

And the more I look, the more
they transpire - blossom almost under
my gaze.

So distant they are, there
in the folds of the comforting sky,
buckled together in wobbly splendour.

As lustrous, my dear, your hair to-day
where it caught the rain,
the drops teeming and jostling each other,
like casual jewels on a fall of velvet.

You are so far beyond my reach,
so sealed, solemn,
beautiful.

Advice on Child-rearing.
(with apologies to R.D. Blackmore, 1825 -1900)

Some need no prodding to be good.
(The gene-pool, if you believe it.)

Some pay no heed as you rant and rave,
Don't be a slob. Don't follow the mob.
Hard to pin down as a blob of mercury.

And some will gently take your face
between their young relentless hands:
the forests, Mum, the Kurds.

So why bang on and try to mould them,
best swallow your words.
They've gone, essentially, no matter

forever stuck at the hip. Point is
the luck -- a daughter bent at the strawberry patch,
then stretching to go and lie in the sun,

the first length swum:
pearls, moon-stones of rarest worth,
to string a life on.

Starting Young

We've shut over the door and ventured out
on the turnpike stair,
concertina'd like Duchamps' leggy nudes
descending.

Goggle-eyed – till light seeps
and gives us the close, the cobbled slope,
and a dog, nosing the small dark
innards of something.

Then it's out on the narrow, murky,
milling streets
where the mill foreman is mustering
his shift.

We hurry along past the bookie's hatch
and the lemonade works shut since
the bombing - at the third one in
of the ten-foot windows the pavement sunders

call down to our mother, lifting between us the loaf
by its ears to show her,
and Uncle Fletch, straight as a column,
standing beside her,
tracking the packet-of-five we belay with a string.

To-day's the furthest from the sun –
Christmas soon.
And after, men in lorries with bits of paper and
mechanical shovels will arrive,
and clear all this away.

The Edinburgh Pigeon

(The summer crowds in Princes Street are sometimes entertained by
a Russian street band.)

He doesn't care one bit for the trumpet's blare,
the flagpole's rattle,
the pavement's scuttle,

he's got other things to think about, Professor Aristotle.

The crowd allows him a clear run, or a strut
you'd say – more like a strut. But say what you like,
the oomphas of brass and bass-

clarinets mean nothing to him. He doesn't

care – just brings to bear his pernickety eye
on the tug-of-war at the niche
in the corner, giving himself over

now and then to rummaging his back.

His students arrive. They dip and veer,
launch their palaeozoic
landing gear – and hump themselves like hooded spies

against sound and weather.

How focussed they are, these neophytes,
following him here, following
him there,

skipping with little fastidious hops

round twiggy heaps
and petroleum streaks in the morning
puddles ....

Are these the same that come up-river
scuppering my dreams
of a handsome lover,

q-r q-r ing, b-r b-r ing at my window-sill?

Are these, when the trumpet finally sounds –
roped together down vertical vaults,
asphalt cracks, stopped-up drains -

the ones to uncover

the forgotten zone, the middle earth,
our abandoned squashed-up
universe?

Clocking Off

The lift-gate bangs and I follow them out,
him in his day kilt, her in jeans,
They cross over towards the corner and I turn
left, make the minutest of adjustments
and shift my shopper between my hands.

It's fine for April - feel how balmy - little barbecue fires
challenging the sky.
The patient traffic loops the loop and I watch the lights;
take dark delight in my constitutional right
to hog the pavement.

Presently, I see one or two I know to nod to,
pick up on my modest windows -
what's up ahead:
an ashtray, flawless, with hand-painted peonies,
my ancient flip-flops on the bedroom floor,
the girl next door, singing.

And, as always, even before I get there, that stir
of bitter-sweetness,
vaguely, in the air.

The Canongait Sonnets

A windless night in cold February and we stood there,
booted and buttoned, the old woman and I,
united by the evening's pleasures. And making his way
up the hill from some great debate,
came a Great Man, stripey scarf and all: *Well, ladies,*
where have you been? giving his indivisible
attention - *And here are others. You've all been?*
Well, well, I'm sorry I missed that.

But I didn't, and wouldn't have, not even for Cicero:
the sovereign verse, sloping street, the church all lit up
and the hour still gilded with triumphant splendour -
a concatenation really. Then the bus came,
blunting the edge, and we, so lately one in all our little
gathered souls, went each our rosy separate way.

Homeward Leg

(Dulce Domum)

Amsterdam falls away. We're time-lagged,
caffeined-out, stare at the befuddled horizon.
And there, just one inch clear,
aloof as the host raised by the priest,
the unruly, mysterious disc of the sun ....

The plane is dropping
level by level.
The wing's cambers are turning to sheen
and the windows pulse
as the lit droplets start scurrying across
and get sluiced away.

Ladeez an gentleMen, tirty-five on the ground,
it commonces to rrain.
There – I'm glad, happy,
                              content to be home.

Changing Rory

(South Hemlock and Haystack Rock, Cannon Beach, Oregon)

He fixes me unblinkingly, one arm a crescent around
  his head.

I kneel at his feet and he twists to see
  the cat-sized gull that flapped down a moment ago
    on the balcony rail.

The adhesive tabs snap into place and he starts to wriggle.
  Lily,Lily,Lily the radio warbles as the blue Pacific's battle-lines
    pull up on the shore.

A piggy-back down to the water-line and freckled feet became
  mottled silver. A minute more, he's soaked through
    and hung from an arm, back and front, like a spiked fish.

My eyelids prickle and I stash it away – this giant's coast,
  where flagfuls of stars and stripes go seething upwards
    on the spiralling thermals. Where a Rock

communes with its ancient past. And an ocean rolls
  into a baby's reach.

No shale or banks like the east coast of Scotland,
  no geese crossing sunlit firths,

but mile upon mile of perfect vees the waves
  have etched on the flat sand.

He takes my hand as we go back. Looks up
  and grins. We grin together,
    but I'm far from home.

All Hallows' Eve

This day that crowns my favourite month
of yellow leaves and turning trees,
of early dark and ponds that freeze
before the winter's well begun,
with groups, scarves wound around their eyes,
who dress in guise of witch and ghoul,
whose lanterns bob by churchyard walls
and congregate in country halls of grey
and green, while childhood hops from foot
to foot, apple-cheeked and half-bemused,
for all its dreams still polarised
between wish and truth –
too soon it comes, the thin candles leak
and shrink, each year too soon
the delegation entering in
as at a ball, in mask and cloak,
to kick up heels as clean
as bone and dance among the crowd unseen.

"Nighthawks", by Edward Hopper
(The Art Institute of Chicago)

He has set the stage so carefully – the street-lines
straight and clean, the windows of the shops
quite bare, and side-by-side, gleamingly,
the two metal coffee-urns standing guard. It's an odyssey.
He must find the bitter colours and a ruthlessness
of light. The images are revealed to him

only to make possible some fulfilment of his own –
window-blinds halfway down across the street,
drinks grown cold, the contemplation of a cigarette
that's just been lit.
See the outcome that's been realised here: a grave couple
side by side, news that will never come.

New York – Tableau Vivant

Tuxedo,
narrow necktie,
hip as pivot,
he plots a path through the gossiping crowd.
Works the room.

You follow and witness a master:
taking an elbow,
mouth at an ear,
he prises a senator out of a huddle,
like a bead from an oyster.

His smile is vast. He never fails,
from every tail can pluck the sting.
This charm thing's
a family thing,
it's sex for him. Nourishing and then gone.

The trees outside are deeply green. Stars appear.
The flags unfurl in silent clamour.
He watches,
then turning,
heads for the bar.

This is the man who sniffed the wind, skirted
the maelstrom. Left the plastered dead
behind him.
This is the Odysseus who walked out of the sea.

High-rise, Ann Street: home

The sky is loaded this sleepy evening,
mauve mixed in with violet, river-blue.
Swallows are flying against the light and people
blur, the distance from here
disfiguring them.

Heat rises. The lift of air laps the gloaming
and wraps the Bridge with the smell of the city.
The great Tay ebbs, adhibits its marks
on the surfacing sand.

All thought slips down
the trenched abysses, coagulates in the dark.

Vestigia

Look, his footprints. Heels faint, hardly
touching the ground -
must have been running,

then over here, at the front of the garden,
the stride shortens,

snow's scuffed where he's slithered round,
eyes screwed up – pure joy in the blinding sunlight.

And up on the dyke, by the bottom gate,
where his winter trainers have scraped the moss,

see, hooded against the wind-force,
he's watching for the Ford Fiesta ....

Each one a gift, like the sole-prints left
on an ancient shore.

How clear they are, etched in the ice –
clipping the light, reflecting the sun.

Come, follow them to the edge of the grass.

Sly Moon

The night settles its belly cautiously,
gingerly. Tendrils flick the bars of the gate.
I lie in wait.

The shadowed clock creeps, slows,
goes deep down
and deeper.

No star-shine
or sails on the horizon –
only a convergence of sea and sky.

And then it rises, crooked, high;
and casements, hatches, chimney-heads
rapturously open their hoards of silver.

The sea turns on its side
sighing, sighing - surrendering its head
on the strewn shore.

The centre shifts; and sleep
and sly promiscuous moon importune
my bed, spread

my body. The tide fills.

The Ode to Joy

On the balcony at St. Joseph's School, peering past
the medal-winners boxed behind the civic heads,
I can make them out: my eldest, scared,
her lanky sister in the band, bored to death, scrunching
her chair, fiddling her hair – at last the moment,
and the Ode to Joy is scraping off her cello string...

And the next thing, under my thighs a Triumph bike
guns; two shadows tilt, hip-to-hip. A moon
climbs; vineyards ahead. The spool
unwinds a year, a river – all really there ever was.
And now this pearl, this perfectly smooth little world,
drops in my lap.
Home, I park it pillow-deep. It clings -
seeds like crazy in the dark.

Birthday Poem, March 2015

Count them off finger
by finger
world's wonders
hills of Rome
the ancients' seven sure-footed ones
that make their way in the deep
empyrean
the candles' shine
on the keys of a kingdom:
the notch on the bone.
Yours to discover

the seventh sin
and the seventh heaven
that will carry you safe on a flowing
ribbon
the welling self
the coils to the panting heart
of the labyrinth.
And alongside ever
the goblins' song
in the snow-white wood
that makes you brave and strong and good.

Count the colours true
as you can
carmine nature's virescent
blue
and mix in your eye
the other four.
Faithful Sir Hamish
brave as a lion
already one
of my seven
Samurai.

Venus Mars magenta cyan
Mercury's white,
the yellows of Saturn.

The Art of Silverpoint

Snail sets its snout to the ground
in aqueous weather.
Slicks and licks
its delicate seam through the lie
of the land.

So, the stylus
drawing along its streak of silver –
a hair's breadth,
the merest whisker.
How risky the business,

how shrewd
the tether.
To be or be absent,
that is the question. The line seizes.

The words shine.

Cento

(After Sappho, Fragment 58)

Oh, but once, once, we were
like young deer,
    wild deer
in the wild wood,

like the hare, pumped up
to the tips of his ears,
    leaping
        the furrows,

or the lark,
oblivious, hunting
    the sun,
 bursting with joy.

Oh, young we were, young
beyond all - but on the horizon,
    the bugle-call,
    clearsounding.

Were my knowing then, my knowing
now, what bliss in the drift of
    the wildwood,
what wild in the wooing.

Notes

Man c. 1492 (p.17)
In September 1513, the Portuguese Vasco da Balbao crossed the Isthmus of Panama from Darien and saw the Pacific, the first European to do so (not stout Cortez as Keats has it). The proximity of this date to Leonardo's drawing prompted the poem.

Callum Innes (p.23)
Ochre on Black (Scottish National Gallery of Modern Art)

The Canongait Sonnets (p.43)
After a reading of Shakespeare sonnets. References are to sonnets 33, 56 and 116.

The Art of Silverpoint (p.54)
The stylus as drawing tool. The metal point, made of silver, brass or bronze, required a drawing surface covered with an applied ground, usually of lead white with a binding solution of glue or gum arabic. Very delicate, precise draftsmanship was needed as the strokes could not be erased or corrected. Exponents included Van Eyck, Durer, Raphael, Leonardo and later George Grosz. Antecedent of the graphite pencil.

Lightning Source UK Ltd.
Milton Keynes UK
UKHW011808110319
338925UK00001B/107/P

9 780993 503573